# 10 WAYS TO USE LESS ENERGY

by Lisa Amstutz

PEBBLE
a capstone imprint

Published by Pebble, an imprint of Capstone
1710 Roe Crest Drive, North Mankato, Minnesota 56003
capstonepub.com

Copyright © 2024 by Capstone. All rights reserved. No part of this publication may be reproduced in whole or in part, or stored in a retrieval system, or transmitted in any form or by any means, electronic, mechanical, photocopying, recording, or otherwise, without written permission of the publisher.

Library of Congress Cataloging-in-Publication Data is available on the Library of Congress website.

ISBN: 9780756577940 (hardcover)
ISBN: 9780756578022 (paperback)
ISBN: 9780756577988 (ebook PDF)

Summary: Do you have any idea how much energy you waste each year? Help save energy, money, and the environment all at the same time with these 10 simple steps and added hands-on activity. Find out what tips work for you and spread the word. Together, we can make a difference!

Editorial Credits
Editor: Mandy R. Robbins; Designer: Heidi Thompson; Media Researcher: Jo Miller; Production Specialist: Tori Abraham

Image Credits
Capstone Studio: Karon Dubke, 11; Getty Images: Ariel Skelley, 7, Cavan Images, 5, Ciaran Griffin, 12, Elva Etienne, 19, John Giustina, 15, Jose Luis Pelaez, 14, Juan Maria Coy Vergara, 8, kate_sept2004, Cover (bottom right), ktaylorg, 16, Marko Geber, 17, SouthWorks, 18; Shutterstock: Africa Studio, Cover (top right), airphoto.gr, 9, Andrii Spy_k, 13, Chubykin Arkady, Cover (bottom left), Iammotos, 6, Krakenimages.com, 10, LeManna, Cover (top left), New Africa, 21

All internet sites appearing in back matter were available and accurate when this book was sent to press.

Printed and bound in China. 5593

# TABLE OF CONTENTS

What Is Energy?................................................................................ 4

How We Use Energy ....................................................................... 6

Energy Problems............................................................................. 8

10 Ways You Can Use Less Energy ........................................10

Activity: Go on an Energy Hunt ...............................................20

    Glossary ........................................................................22

    Read More ...................................................................23

    Internet Sites ..............................................................23

    Index...............................................................................24

    About the Author .....................................................24

Words in **BOLD** are in the glossary.

# WHAT IS ENERGY?

Flip! You turn on a switch. Your light comes on. But how?

Under that switch are wires. They carry **energy** to the light bulb. That makes it come on.

Energy is the ability to do work. It can move things. Heat and light are forms of energy. So is electricity.

# HOW WE USE ENERGY

It's a school day! Your alarm rings. You pop in some toast. Then, maybe you get a ride. All of these things take energy.

Energy heats and cools your home. It makes cars and buses go. It runs the stove, microwave, and fridge. It runs the washer and dryer too.

# ENERGY PROBLEMS

Some energy comes from the sun, water, or wind. These **resources** are **renewable**. That means they will not run out.

Other energy comes from **fossil fuels**. Oil, gas, and coal are in this group. These fuels have many uses. But one day, they may run out. Burning them can **pollute** the air too. It can harm the planet.

# 10 WAYS YOU CAN USE LESS ENERGY

1. Brrr! It's a chilly day. You could turn up the heat. Or you could wrap up in a blanket. Which would use less energy? The blanket!

**2.** Be sure to close the door when you leave home. We use energy to heat and cool our homes. Don't waste that energy.

**3.** Phones and TVs use energy. So do computers. Turn them off when you're done with them. Or look for other ways to have fun.

4. When you finish using a charger, unplug it. It's easy to forget. Put a sticky note on the cord to remind you!

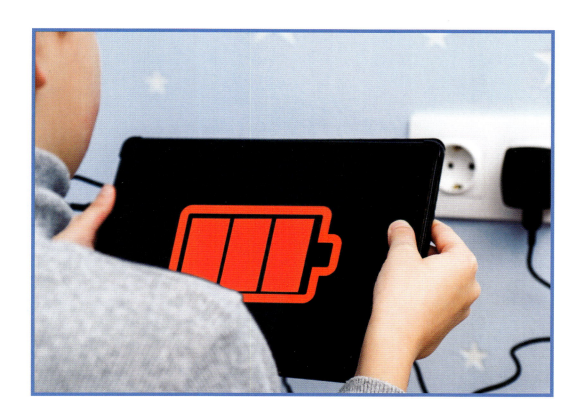

**5.** Need a cold drink? Be quick. Don't let the fridge door hang open. It takes energy to cool down again.

**6.** Doing laundry takes energy too. Hang wet laundry on a clothesline. That way you don't need to run the dryer.

**7.** Can you walk to school or to the park? Most vehicles use a lot of fuel. Walk or bike when you can.

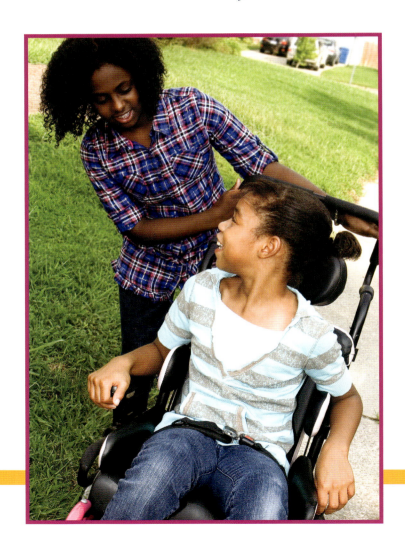

**8.** You can save energy by riding a bus or train too. They can carry many people at a time.

**9.** Leaving a room? Turn off the light! It only takes a second, and it saves energy.

**10.** As a class or a family, write to leaders in your state. Tell them you want a cleaner planet. Ask them to change laws. Tell them to choose clean energy.

No one person can save the environment. But we can all do our part. Your words can help make a change!

# ACTIVITY: GO ON AN ENERGY HUNT

Saving energy can be fun. You and your family can make a game of it. Walk around your home. See who can find the most energy wasters. Look for lights or TVs left on. Write down what you find.

# GLOSSARY

**energy** (EH-nuhr-jee)—the ability to do work, such as moving things or giving heat or light

**fossil fuel** (FAH-suhl FYOOL)—a natural fuel formed from the remains of plants and animals; coal, oil, and natural gas are fossil fuels

**pollute** (puh-LOOT)—to make something dirty or unsafe

**renewable** (ri-NOO-uh-buhl)—able to be restored or replaced by natural sources

**resource** (REE-sorss)—something useful or valuable to a place or person

## READ MORE

DiOrio, Rana. *What Does It Mean to Be Green?* Naperville, IL: Little Pickle Press, 2021.

Gaertner, Meg. *Saving Energy*. Mendota Heights, MN: Little Blue House, 2022.

Gleisner, Jenna Lee. *Let's Save Energy!* Minneapolis: Jump!, 2019.

## INTERNET SITES

*10 Ways to Save Energy for Children*
twinkl.com/blog/10-ways-to-save-energy-for-children

*Energy Kids*
eia.gov/kids/

*NASA: Climate Kids*
climatekids.nasa.gov/menu/energy/

# INDEX

cooling, 7, 11, 14

electricity, 4
electronics, 12, 13, 20

fuels, 9, 16

heating, 4, 7, 10, 11

laundry, 7, 15
laws, 19
lights, 4, 18, 20

pollution, 9

renewable resources, 8

switches, 4

vehicles, 6, 7, 16, 17

# ABOUT THE AUTHOR

Lisa Amstutz is the author of more than 150 children's books on topics ranging from applesauce to zebra mussels. An ecologist by training, she enjoys sharing her love of nature with kids. Lisa lives on a small farm with her family.